The Tigers' Tale

Catherine Barr

Illustrated by
Tara Anand

BLOOMSBURY
CHILDREN'S BOOKS
LONDON OXFORD NEW YORK NEW DELHI SYDNEY

Tiger tiger, burning bright

With their flame-coloured coats and amber eyes, tigers are mysterious, majestic and exceptionally powerful.

There are more wild tigers in India than anywhere else on Earth. Legends about the Royal Bengal tiger are woven into the country's long history. Yet tigers here, and everywhere, have always been vulnerable.

For hundreds of years, these iconic animals have been cruelly hunted by poachers – people who illegally kill wild animals – causing their numbers to dangerously dwindle. But it was not until 1975 that all tigers were finally declared an endangered species. There were once nine types of tiger, but three are already extinct.

Despite this, people are still killing tigers and destroying the wild places where they live.

Once, over 100,000 tigers prowled forests and grasslands across Asia. Today, less than 4,000 tigers roam free. Humans are pushing these magnificent beasts to the brink of extinction.

We must ensure that the fiery elegance of the tiger will forever burn bright.

How can we save them?

Prologue
The Emerald Forest

This tale unfolds in Panna, Central India, a dusty landscape that transforms into an Emerald Forest.

For much of the year, Panna's rolling hills of dry forest, high grasslands and hidden gorges bake in relentless sun. But with the arrival of monsoon rains Panna comes to life, dripping in shiny shades of green. The swollen waters of the Ken River crash over towering waterfalls as the river snakes through the reserve.

From the ground to the sky, Panna bursts with life. Antelopes, gazelles and deer graze on the high plains. Porcupines shuffle through deep bushes. Leopards and sloth bears lounge amongst shady trees and tiny rusty-spotted cats slink through the dark forest at night. Snakes ripple across the forest floor and crocodiles slink along the banks of the river and surrounding marshes.

More than 300 species of birds circle the hazy skies. Graceful woolly-necked storks, scavenging vultures, colourful plum-headed parakeets and paradise flycatchers all make the Emerald Forest of Panna their home.

It's not only wildlife that thrives in this wild, beautiful place. People and cattle also live close to the reserve boundaries, relying on the forest for food and fuel.

But of all these spectacular species, it is the tiger who rules the land.

Panna became a National Park in 1981. Later in 1994, it became India's 22nd tiger reserve – a protected area created for the conservation of tigers. It became illegal to kill wildlife and destroy precious tiger habitats. Yet, for many years, there were very few tigers in the reserve and little was known about them. So, in 1996, a team of scientists came to Panna to study its tigers.

They set out to gather information that could help protect tigers in India and around the world.

Meet the tigers

Many grand tigers have padded across Panna's plains. But scientists in this story followed the tales of two extraordinary tiger dynasties.

The first dynasty

M-91
This magnificent male tiger ruled Panna alone for five years.

Hairy Foot
A huge tiger with particularly hairy feet, who is at first mysterious and difficult to find.

52
With distinctive markings on her forehead bearing the numbers 5 and 2, this female tiger became the Queen of Panna for many years.

Sayani
Sayani is the daughter of M-91 and 52.

Julie
Julie is mother to Madla's first cubs inside Panna Tiger Reserve.

T3
A lone male with a strong homing instinct.

Madla
Madla strolled into Panna in 1996, and went on to rule the east of the reserve.

T1
An orphan female tiger born in Bandhavgarn Tiger Reserve. 'T' stands for tiger.

The second dynasty

T2
Another female orphan, T2 had 14 cubs with T3.

T4 and T5
Orphaned when they were just a year and a half, these two female tigers were brought to Panna from Kahna Tiger Reserve.

Counting tigers

Tigers are shy and roam huge distances, often cloaked in darkness. So how do scientists find and track them? It all begins with counting paws and stripes …

Searching for pugmarks

For many years, people counted tigers by looking for their footprints. They made a plaster cast of these 'pugmarks' to identify individual tigers. It can be difficult to tell tigers apart because their prints look different in wet or dry mud, so it's easy to make mistakes. The same tiger's footprint can be collected from different places and counted as a new tiger each time.

Setting camera traps

Nowadays, one of the most reliable ways to count tigers is to take photographs, as each tiger's stripes are unique. Waterproof camera traps are set on either side of familiar trails and triggered every time an animal strolls by. In India more than 10,000 camera traps capture these 'tiger selfies' in the wild.

Project Tiger

By finding out how many tigers live in the park and how they behave, scientists can give forest guards, local communities and governments information that will help protect tigers.

In 1973, the Indian Government launched a conservation plan called Project Tiger to save Royal Bengal tigers from extinction, so counting them became very important. But as you will discover as our story unfolds, the numbers didn't always add up and many, many tigers disappeared …

Tigers are fitted with collars to help people track them using radio signals. These alert scientists if a tiger strays into danger outside a protected area and they can warn villagers if a tiger comes too close.

PART ONE: The first dynasty

Madla (1996)

It's dawn and an enormous tiger emerges from the forest. Soft stripes ripple across the early morning sun. He pads across red earth, leaving huge pugmarks in the dust.

Who is this grand tiger? Where has he come from and where is he going? Nobody knows. He has never been seen in M-91's territory before. To find out more about him, a scientist and a skilled vet must fit him with a radio collar so they can track him through the thick forest.

To follow this magnificent cat, the scientist and vet travel on the backs of elephants. The elephants are each guided by a 'mahout', a local elephant trainer. Together the team begin to search, bumping quietly through the forest.

At last, they see a flicker of stripes amongst the trees. The tiger ignores the approaching elephant. But the elephant fidgets, nervous of the fearsome predator close by.

The vet must fire a tranquilliser dart that will put the tiger to sleep for enough time to fit the radio collar. He is a good shot and easily hits his mark. The team wait for ten minutes to make sure the dart has worked.

Madla

First, the scientist cautiously climbs down from his elephant – he has just twenty minutes before this tiger wakes up. He gives its tail a tug. Nothing. Confident that the tranquilliser has taken effect, the rest of the team climb off their elephants and fit the collar carefully around the tiger's huge neck. It is dangerous work and they must be quick.

To wake him, the scientists give him an injection. Afterwards, they have only minutes to scramble to safety on the elephants' backs. A tiger's hearing comes back first, so a scientist's clap brings the sleepy tiger up on to unsteady paws. He slinks back into the bushes.

They name him Madla. *Beep beep.* **His new collar tells scientists he is on the move.**

Tiger queens

**Madla is confident, dominant and extremely large.
But he is not alone … A watchful female tiger
is on the prowl.**

This forest is her home – she is the Queen of Panna. Black hairs on her brow curl into the numbers 5 and 2, making her instantly recognisable. The scientsits name her 52.

She is far away from the big new male Madla, but she is nursing cubs and becomes anxious when she senses him on the reserve. Sometimes a new male tiger will kill a female's cubs if they are not his own. 52 must be alert to protect her young.

This is 52's second litter and their father is M-91, the old male tiger who patrols the west of the reserve. He and 52 have several daughters from their previous litter. These females are young, but strong and fiercely independent.

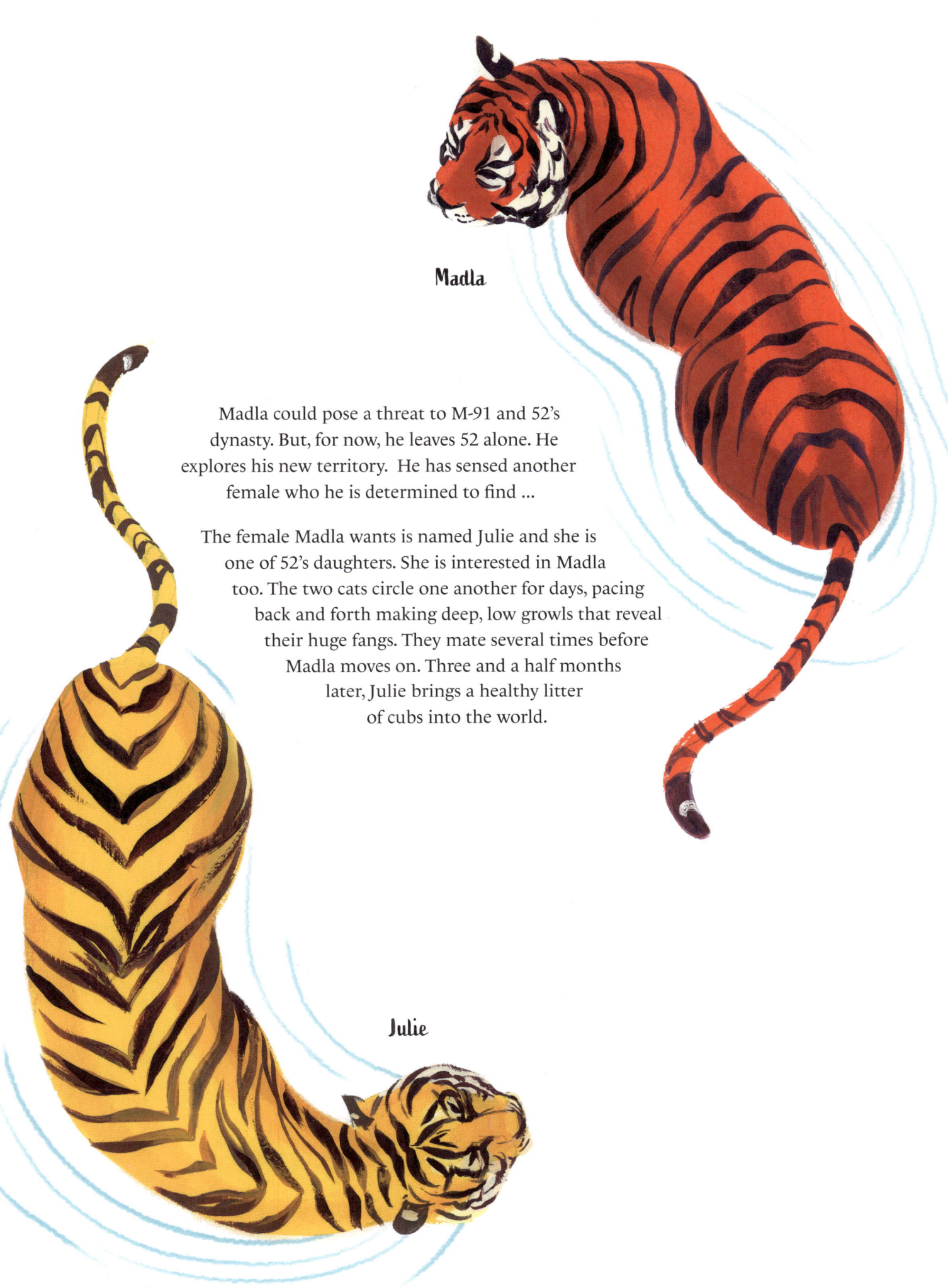

Madla

Madla could pose a threat to M-91 and 52's dynasty. But, for now, he leaves 52 alone. He explores his new territory. He has sensed another female who he is determined to find …

The female Madla wants is named Julie and she is one of 52's daughters. She is interested in Madla too. The two cats circle one another for days, pacing back and forth making deep, low growls that reveal their huge fangs. They mate several times before Madla moves on. Three and a half months later, Julie brings a healthy litter of cubs into the world.

Julie

A clash of pride (1997)

Madla has a mate now, but he is restless …

He marks his boundaries, spraying and scraping. He walks thirty kilometres each day and rarely stops. He is the busiest tiger the scientists have ever seen. At night and in the early evening, he slinks through the dusty vegetation, travelling through villages in and on the edge of the reserve.

Mostly Madla avoids M-91 and keeps to the east of the reserve. And, for a while, it seems like they live in harmony. But one day Madla crosses an invisible line into the west, trespassing on territory that is not his own.

Madla and M-91 finally meet. They snarl and spit. Face to face at last, their eyes lock and they dip their heads. A fierce, deadly dance is about to begin. With a sudden leap, Madla strikes. But M-91 isn't ready to give up just yet. Both tigers rear up to battle on their powerful hind legs. They crash into each other, rolling in the dust. Their great paws look clumsy, but they hide razor-sharp claws.

M-91

For days they dance warily around each other, growling and waiting for the chance to strike again. Finally, M-91 limps away, wounded and exhausted. He has lost most of his territory, but he cannot fight any longer. Madla has won. Panna has a new tiger king.

For three years Madla rules the reserve.

But big cats' territories ebb and flow, and there are other tigers nearby who could take his crown …

Hairy Foot (2000)

One day, the scientists discover a new tiger footprint, or pugmark, in the dust. It is unlike any they have seen before.

Looking closely at the pugmark, scientists can see the marks of thick hairs on the front pads of the feet. Another big male tiger. They name him Hairy Foot.

It is not unusual for other tigers to pad across the borders into other tiger territories. Rivals come and go. Some are 'floaters' – tigers passing through while others choose to stay. But week after week hairy footprints appear on Panna's paths … This tiger seems determined to stay.

What does this mean for Madla? Will he have to fight off another male to keep his territory? Not at first. It seems Madla and Hairy Foot share Panna in peace. Madla continues to roam in the east, while Hairy Foot takes the west.

The scientists want to know everything about Hairy Foot. But there's a problem … they can't find him! Day after day and night after night, bumping along dirt tracks and staring down binoculars to scan the forest, they look. Yet this huge tiger hides from view.

Eventually, a camera trap catches Hairy Foot on film. But without a radio collar it is almost impossible for scientists to find him and study his behaviour.

They must find a different way to track this invisible tiger …

Camera trap

Hairy Foot

Sayani and cubs

A female tiger finally helps scientists unravel Hairy Foot's story.

As they search for Hairy Foot, the scientists listen for signs of other tigers who already wear radio collars. Soon, they detect a signal from a female they know well – Sayani, one of 52's daughters. The beep gets louder and clearer, and finally they find Sayani sheltering in the shadows of a cave. Sinking onto cool, shaded rock, her side heaves with a steady breath.

After hours of quiet observation through cameras and binoculars, a tiny bundle of fluffy stripes topples into view. The scientists marvel as Sayani bends her mighty head to lick her cub with a rough tongue. Another cub then emerges from the shadows of the cave, clambering over his mother to find warmth and milk. Sayani is a patient mother. She will look after her precious family for more than a year.

The scientists wonder if Hairy Foot is the father of the cubs. Although he cannot be seen, he may be close by.

At last the scientists find Hairy Foot sprawled across the rocks not far from the cave. He must be the father of these cubs. The family role of male tigers is not well understood, so the tiger team is fascinated to watch and learn as Sayani relaxes and Hairy Foot lingers.

The peace of this tiger family ripples across the reserve.

Swimming in cool waters

Wide and glittering blue, the Ken River tumbles over Panna's famously high waterfalls, plunging into shady pools.

Prey and predators in Panna rely on the Ken River all year round. The clear, unpolluted waters are home to a whole host of wildlife. Silver fish twist and turn below the surface. Tropical birds nest on the riverbanks and antelope, wild dogs and monkeys dip their heads in to take a refreshing drink.

And, of course, there are the tigers. Tigers like water. The forest pools and streams are the perfect places to cool down from the searing heat and shake off biting insects.

Sayani takes her cubs to these cool places and sinks down into the calm waters. The cubs splash and play around their gentle mother. With webbed feet unlike any other in the cat family, tigers are natural swimmers, instantly at home in the water.

Long summers pass with plentiful water, shelter and food. Tigers flourish and breed. By 2002, seven females in Panna have had litters. Five of these tigers were fitted with a radio collar, so their movements, behaviour and families were tracked to understand what they needed to thrive. What was happening in Panna became the world's best-documented tiger success story, with detailed scientific notes providing insight for scientists all over the world.

All was well. But later that year, things began to change …

Vanishing tigers

By 2002, tigers in Panna had began to mysteriously disappear.

As time passed, it became more difficult to catch a tiger on camera and even their radio collars stopped transmitting signals.

It wasn't long before scientists discovered traps hidden in the vegetation near waterholes. This showed that poachers were lurking nearby, putting tigers in serious danger.

Full of fear, the scientists searched for the tigers they knew. And then, one dark day, a soft striped body was discovered by local villagers.

Radio collar

Too late

Dusty leaves blew over Sayani, the body of the great tiger mother.

Days before, the signal from Sayani's radio collar had shown that she'd wandered close to a village at the edge of the reserve, putting herself and her cubs in danger. The scientists knew where she was, but getting there meant crossing hilly, rough ground. Only an elephant's strong feet could help them find Sayani.

The team asked the managers of the reserve if they could use an elephant to help find Sayani. But the managers refused and said elephants were for tourists, not scientists. The scientists pleaded – Sayani was in danger! Frustrating days passed until finally the managers were persuaded to change their minds. But it was too late.

To the scientists' great sadness, Sayani had died in a snare that poachers had set for deer. Her cubs had gone. Lost and alone, they probably died without their mother. Tragically, this young tiger family could have been saved if the scientists had been able to help.

Then six months later, in June 2003, the great male, Hairy Foot was found dead in a well. His strange death has never been explained.

By now, Sayani's mother, 52, was old and unlikely to have more cubs. Her daughters were the only hope for the future of tigers in Panna. But unchallenged in the silence of the night, poachers stole the tigers of Panna Tiger Reserve. Every last one.

By 2009, there was not a single tiger left in the Emerald Forest.

The Panna tragedy unfolds

How did this tiger success story turn to tragedy?

In 2000, the people in charge of the park changed. New managers made it harder for scientists to track the tigers because …

Elephants were only used for tourists

In the remote Panna landscape, scientists need elephants to keep track of tigers. If they know where tigers are, then it is easier to keep villages safe and watch out for poachers nearby.

Scientists' repeated warnings of poaching were ignored

Scientists warned that this illegal hunting was becoming an increasing threat to wildlife and tigers in Panna. But no action was taken.

Reserve boundaries were poorly patrolled

Most tiger reserves are unfenced so animals can move freely in the wider landscape. But if the boundaries of these protected areas are poorly patrolled, poachers creep across these invisible lines.

The scientists were told to leave

The scientists, who had so much useful knowledge and love for tigers in the reserve, were suddenly told to leave and stop their important work.

But perhaps the strangest and biggest concern was that the managers of Panna Tiger Reserve at this time denied that tigers were vanishing at all …

And Panna was not the only reserve in India where tigers disappeared.

Project Tiger was failing.

The number of tigers in India was falling fast.

PART TWO: Threats To Tigers

The illegal wildlife trade

One of the biggest threats to the survival of wild tigers is poaching for the illegal wildlife trade.

Wild tigers are killed for their skins, teeth, claws and bones, which are then sold to international traders. People pay high prices for tiger skins and parts – they are used as symbols of wealth and as ingredients in traditional medicine.

The tiger traders often tempt poor local people with money to become poachers, so it is important that villages close to reserves benefit from tigers in other ways. For example, by hosting wildlife tourists or having jobs as forest guards.

Tigers are supposed to be safe in tiger reserves and national parks because these places are protected. But it can be difficult for guards to patrol the long, unfenced boundaries and poachers creep in. Under the cover of darkness, they steal through tiger forests on a mission to kill.

Most tigers are hard to find, so how do poachers catch them?

A hungry tiger will stay close to prey it has killed for days to feed. This makes the tiger vulnerable because a poacher can poison its food or snare the tiger. Poachers are careful and cruel. They know that a gunshot wound will damage the tiger's coat, reducing its price to a rich buyer.

Protecting tigers from poachers depends heavily on the people in charge of the tiger reserve. If people use reliable scientific knowledge, employ dedicated guards who patrol for poachers with the support of local communities, tigers will breed and their numbers will rise.

Captivity

Although the numbers of wild tigers are falling rapidly, there are more than 12,000 tigers kept captive in cages around the world. Incredibly, that's about triple the number of wild tigers.

Tiger farms

Poachers hunt and sell wild tigers, but that's not the only way their body parts are sold. Many tigers are raised in 'tiger farms' and eventually killed for their claws, paws, teeth and skin. This is illegal in most countries, but tragically, it does still happen.

Tigers for entertainment

Sadly, there are hundreds of 'zoos' or so-called animal sanctuaries around the world where tigers are forced to entertain humans. In these grim places, tigers are dragged out for tourist selfies and 'shows'. They often live in cruel, cramped conditions.

Pet tigers

Tigers are also kept as exotic pets. Pacing tiny cages in gardens and yards, as many as 5,000 tigers live in cruel conditions in private zoos and homes in the USA alone. These tigers are forced to live close to humans without freedom to use their natural instincts to hunt, patrol territories and raise a wild tiger family.

People around the world are working together to shut down tiger farms, to end the international tiger trade and to stop people keeping tigers as exotic pets. But there is still a lot of work to be done.

Habitat loss

Tigers live best in huge rolling landscapes of grassland and forest. But these habitats are shrinking. In fact, almost all of the land where tigers once roamed has disappeared. Forests have been cut down and land has been farmed or built on. At least half of India's 52 tiger reserves have been sliced up by new roads and railways, been damaged by mines and dams or surrounded by farms and villages. This forces tigers to live closer to humans and suffer the conflict this can bring.

Nature's balance

At dusk, the calls of monkeys and deer echo through the trees in the Emerald Forest, warning that the tigers are on the hunt. But although these animals fear tigers, they depend on them to survive. If tigers disappear, the number of prey increases rapidly. These extra animals eat more and more vegetation, which changes the habitat. Some plants and trees struggle to grow and many animal homes are lost. The connection between animals, plants and people in one place is called an ecosystem.

An emerald ecosystem

Tiger forests are important in slowing down climate change, caused by human activities that add lots of carbon dioxide to our air. Trees take carbon dioxide from the air when they use sunlight to make their food and store it in their trunks, roots and branches.

Forest loss fuels climate change
When trees are cut down, carbon is released back into the air. This adds to climate change, which is warming the planet and threatening the survival of most life on Earth. So preserving tiger forests is important in protecting our planet.

People depend on healthy forests
Forests filter pollution from rainwater and the network of tree roots stop soil from slumping into streams. Soil also reduces the risk of flooding by soaking water up like a sponge. If forests are destroyed to build roads, mines or dams, rivers can become polluted and there is less clean water for people to drink.

To protect tigers and their important role as top predators, it is critical to protect wild places where they live.

PART THREE: The second dynasty
New tigers in an ancient place

Panna needed a new tiger family, so in 2009 tiger experts made an ambitious plan.

First, two female tigers, named T1 and T2, were brought to Panna. It was hoped that they could mother a new generation of tigers. But first, they'd need a male to mate with …

Tiger scientists wondered where to find a new male tiger for Panna. Working together they found a strong five-year-old in Pench Tiger Reserve, which is 400 kilometres south of Panna. He was named T3.

Unfortunately, convincing T3 to make Panna his home was a challenge! After just ten days slinking through the bushes and rolling in the long grass, T3 began to head south … out of the reserve. Where was he going?

Some people believe a 'homing instinct' was driving T3 back to the place from where he'd come. From bears to sea turtles and birds, many animals navigate long journeys to return to the place where they were born or bred.

But Panna needed T3. The team were going to have to come up with a clever plan to persuade this tiger to turn around …

35

Four elephants on your tail

So began an extraordinary game of hide and seek.

A group of 70 people, including forest guards, scientists, local helpers, and skilled mahouts riding elephants all worked together to bring this homesick big cat back to Panna.

But T3 wasn't easy to catch … even with an army of people and four elephants on his tail. An elusive ripple of black and orange, T3 crept through the scrub and between the trees. He hid in tall grass and lingered in the shadows. Eventually, his radio signal appeared.

However, he slipped into the Ken River and paddled out of Panna. Beyond the reserve T3 was unprotected and more vulnerable to poachers. With less wild prey to eat, he was hungry and dangerous too.

Still, the great cat padded on. He wove around remote villages and across fields of lentils, chickpeas and mustard. Now, so close to people, his anxious followers feared he would be shot, snared or poisoned.

They tried everything they could think of to get him to turn around. They lit walls of fires, but T3 wove around them. They banged drums and made loud noises, but T3 wasn't scared. He was just determined to carry on.

Until one day, his desperate followers reluctantly decided to dart him. Once asleep, he was safely transported back to Panna for the second time.

How could this lone wanderer be encouraged to stay this time?

The wee trick

Strangely, the answer to keeping T3 close to home was tiger wee.

Male and female tigers spray their wee at trees, to mark their boundaries and attract mates. For most of us, the smell of urine is disgusting, but tiger wee smells like buttered popcorn!

The scientists collected tiger wee from captive female tigers in Bhopal Zoo in central India – and dripped it in the Emerald Forest. Then, they waited …

The trick worked! Soon enough, T3 male detected the scent of popcorn and followed his nose in search of a mate.

T3 roared and T1 responded to his call. For four days these two tigers formed a close bond … mating and walking together in their new shared territory.

A new tiger story began to unfold. It wasn't long before T1 had four cubs, tiny striped bundles that tumbled over their mother in a shady cave. Two of T1's cubs sadly died at just four months old, but the other two tigers still roam the reserve today. Since then, T1 has given birth to many more litters.

Later that year, T2 mated with T3, who then became a mother of 14 more tigers in the Emerald Forest! Her cubs now roam free over Panna and have families of their own. With the arrival and growth of these new tiger families there is new hope for this precious and important forest predator.

But the offspring of T1, T2 and T3 were not the only new arrivals to Panna …

Raised by hand (2008–2011)

Far away from Panna, there were two young cubs.

They had been orphaned when their mother was killed by a male tiger. Just a year and a half old, they would struggle to survive in the wild alone. But these two were lucky …

Soon after their mother's death, the two cubs were picked up by forest guards at Kanha Tiger Reserve. They were carefully transported to a large enclosure inside the park, where they would grow up under the care of the Kanha team. Following advice from tiger experts, the team encouraged the cubs to learn to look after themselves, with as little human contact as possible.

To survive in the wild, cubs must learn to fear and avoid humans. If they don't, they might be tempted to venture close to villages. It is therefore risky to introduce captive tigers, who have grown up around humans, back into the wild and, at the time in which our story takes place, it had never been done. But the team at Kanha saw an exciting opportunity to help Panna's tiger population grow.

Teams at Panna and Kanha worked together to release the first of these orphan tigers, named T4, in Panna in March 2011. By this point, she was four and a half years old, so old enough to find a mate and have cubs of her own.

The team needed to make sure T4 would accept Panna as her home. They sprayed her wee around the area of the park where she was released, hoping the scent would attract the ruling male, T3.

The two tigers found each other just a few days later. After days spent circling one another, playfully growling and mating, T3 showed T4 how to make her first kill. Soon after, she gathered the courage to hunt alone. But in November 2011, the orphan tigress gave birth to her first litter. The birth became famous – **it was the first time in the world that a hand-reared tiger had been successfully released into the wild and given birth!**

Saving tigers

As the years rolled by, more cubs tumbled into Panna Tiger Reserve.

Today, there may be as many as 30 tigers using the reserve. Tigers are stalking, hunting, playing, lounging on rocks, dozing in caves and slipping into streams in this deep green forest once again. Visitors, though, will be lucky to glimpse a streak of orange rippling through the trees. Tigers are perfectly camouflaged in Panna's deep, dappled shade.

Even with success stories such as Panna's, tigers everywhere still must move with stealth to survive. People with wealth and power are still demanding tiger skins and parts, illegal wildlife dealers are making cruel plans and poachers are lurking in the shadows. Bulldozers and chainsaws are destroying precious habitats, while towns and cities circle shrinking islands of tiger forest.

Happily, in some places like Panna, tiger numbers are rising. But now the Reserve is threatened by plans for a huge dam, which would mean flooding of vital tiger habitat. However, experts and local people are working together to stop this, determined to protect the landscape.

In India, as around the world, making space for wildlife and people is a challenge. But everywhere people are rising up to meet that challenge … and you can help too!

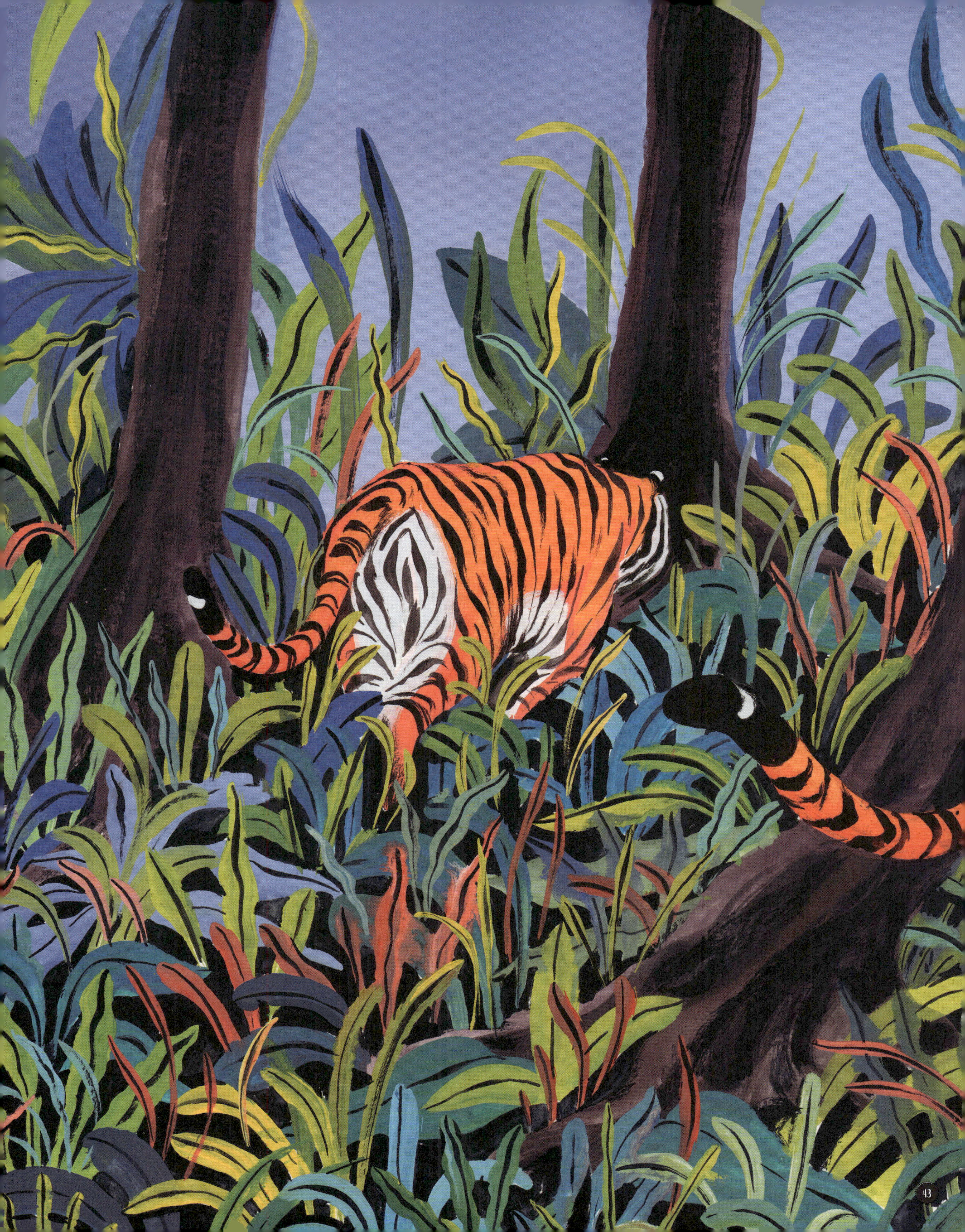

PART FOUR: The future of tigers

Tiger conservation

Around the world thousands of people are fighting to protect tigers and the forests they live in. Everyone has an important part to play, and saving tigers is possible if we work together.

Scientists must accurately count and monitor tiger numbers. By sharing this research with **park managers** and **governments**, they help ensure the right plans are put in place to protect tigers.

Local governments must support tiger conservation plans. This might involve closing roads that run through reserves at night so wildlife can hunt without risk.

Every day millions of people risk walking into tiger forests to collect firewood from trees. When **local governments** and **charities** give these communities gas fires instead, it helps protect people, tigers and the forest.

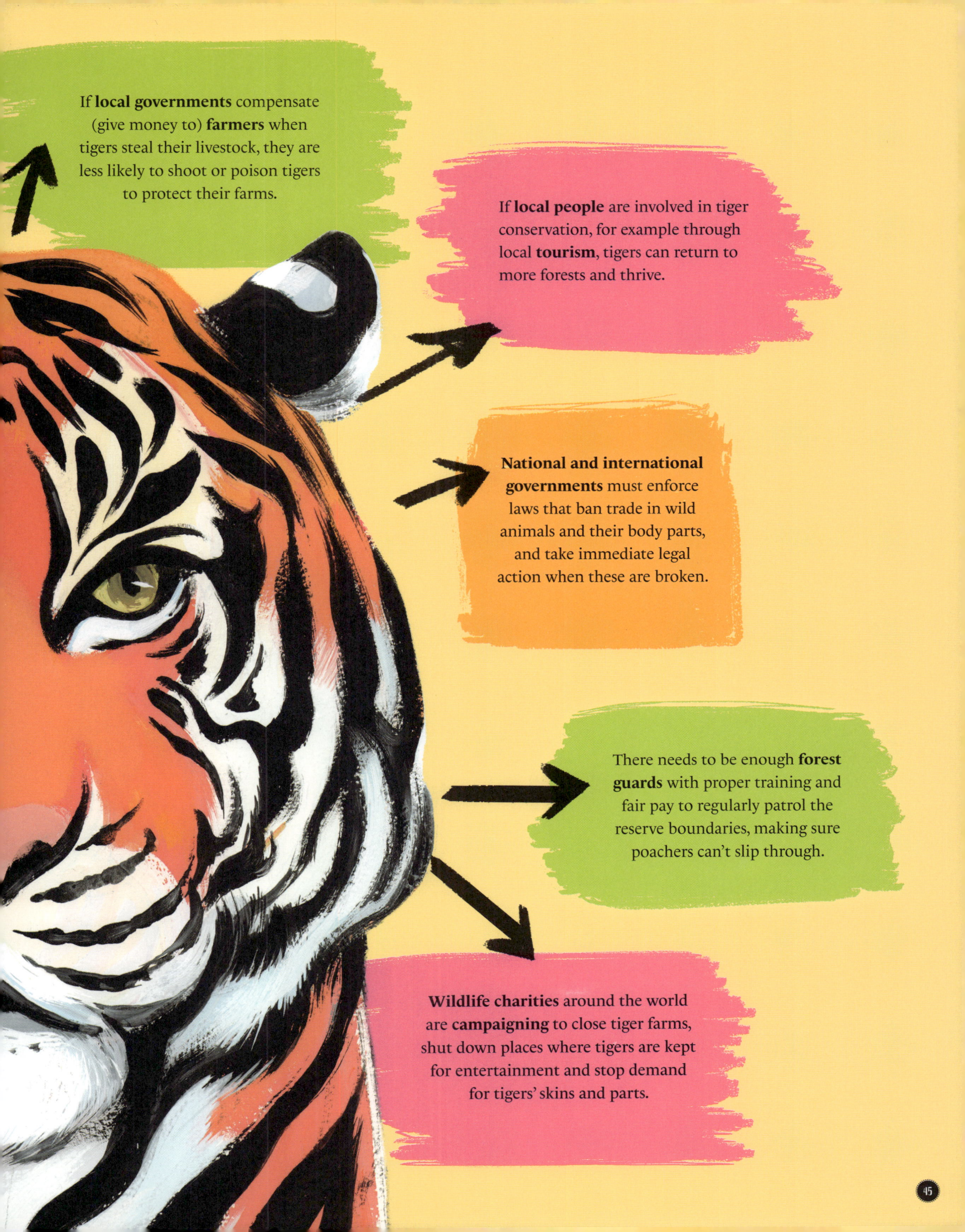

If **local governments** compensate (give money to) **farmers** when tigers steal their livestock, they are less likely to shoot or poison tigers to protect their farms.

If **local people** are involved in tiger conservation, for example through local **tourism**, tigers can return to more forests and thrive.

National and international governments must enforce laws that ban trade in wild animals and their body parts, and take immediate legal action when these are broken.

There needs to be enough **forest guards** with proper training and fair pay to regularly patrol the reserve boundaries, making sure poachers can't slip through.

Wildlife charities around the world are **campaigning** to close tiger farms, shut down places where tigers are kept for entertainment and stop demand for tigers' skins and parts.

How YOU can help tigers

→ **Investigate** and gather facts about tigers that show people why it's important to protect this magnificent species.

→ **Spread the word** by making a poster for your classroom, writing stories about tigers and talking about them with family and friends.

→ **Take action!** If you live in a country with wild tigers, find out what your government is doing to protect them. Even if there aren't wild tigers in your country, you can still write to your local MP and ask them to support campaigns against the illegal wildlife trade in tigers and other endangered animals.

→ **Don't visit so-called tiger sanctuaries** where tigers are 'handled' for entertainment and forced to do tricks, pose for selfies or even taken for walks.

→ **If you visit tiger reserves,** travel with a holiday company which supports local communities involved in tiger conservation because this can really help tigers and the people that live nearby.

→ **Charities and projects** around the world are really making a difference.

Here are some you can support. Be sure to check with an adult before going onto these websites:

Environmental Investigation Agency: investigates illegal trade in tiger parts and skins

eia-international.org

Fauna & Flora International: supports tiger conservation and campaigns to stop illegal wildlife trade

www.fauna-flora.org

Holématthi Nature Foundation (HNF): conserves the wild tiger landscape of Karnataka in the south of India

www.holematthi.org

TRAFFIC: campaigns to end the global wildlife trade

www.traffic.org

WWF: supports global tiger conservation and campaigns to protect tigers all over the world

wwf.panda.org

Together,
we can save
tigers.

Acknowledgements

To Nincha, who showed me my first wild tiger – T.A.

For Mum with love, in admiration of your 'tiger' nickname earned so long ago – C.B.

Author Acknowledgements

With huge thanks to the dedicated tiger experts and scientists in India with whom we collaborated to understand and research this story. Conservation scientist Dr Sanjay Gubbi for sharing his knowledge and experience of studying tigers in Karnataka. Award-winning filmmaker Mike Birkhead for kindly sharing his extraordinary film *Tigers of the Emerald Forest*. Debbie Banks from the Environmental Investigation Agency for expertise on wildlife trade. My friend Sophie Hartman, Founder of Holidays in Rural India who connected me up to a wonderful networks of tiger scientists working in India – and who inspired and organised my visits to Kanha Tiger Reserve, where I first saw a tiger in the wild one Christmas Day.

References:

The Rise and Fall of the Emerald Forest: Ten years of Research in Panna National Park by Raghu Chundawat

Our Tigers Return: The Story of Panna Tiger Reserve (2009-2015) by Rangaiah Sreenivasa Murphy and Peeyush Sekhsaria

Second Nature: saving tiger landscapes in the twenty-first century by Sanjay Gubbi

Film: *Tigers of the Emerald Forest* directed by Mike Birkhead. Mike Birkhead Associates.

Websites listed on page 46 accurate at time of going to print

BLOOMSBURY CHILDREN'S BOOKS
Bloomsbury Publishing Plc
50 Bedford Square, London, WC1B 3DP, UK
29 Earlsfort Terrace, Dublin 2, Ireland

BLOOMSBURY, BLOOMSBURY CHILDREN'S BOOKS and
the Diana logo are trademarks of Bloomsbury Publishing Plc

First published in Great Britain 2023 by Bloomsbury Publishing Plc

Text copyright © Catherine Barr
Illustrations copyright © Tara Anand

Catherine Barr and Tara Anand have asserted their right under the Copyright,
Designs and Patents Act, 1988, to be identified as Author and Illustrator of this work

All rights reserved.
No part of this publication may be reproduced or transmitted in any form
or by any means, electronic or mechanical, including photocopying, recording,
or any information storage or retrieval system, without prior permission
in writing from the publishers

A catalogue record for this book is available from the British Library

ISBN: 9781526626554

2 4 6 8 10 9 7 5 3 1

Printed and bound in China by Leo Paper Products, Heshan, Guangdong

To find out more about our authors and books visit www.bloomsbury.com and sign up for our newsletters

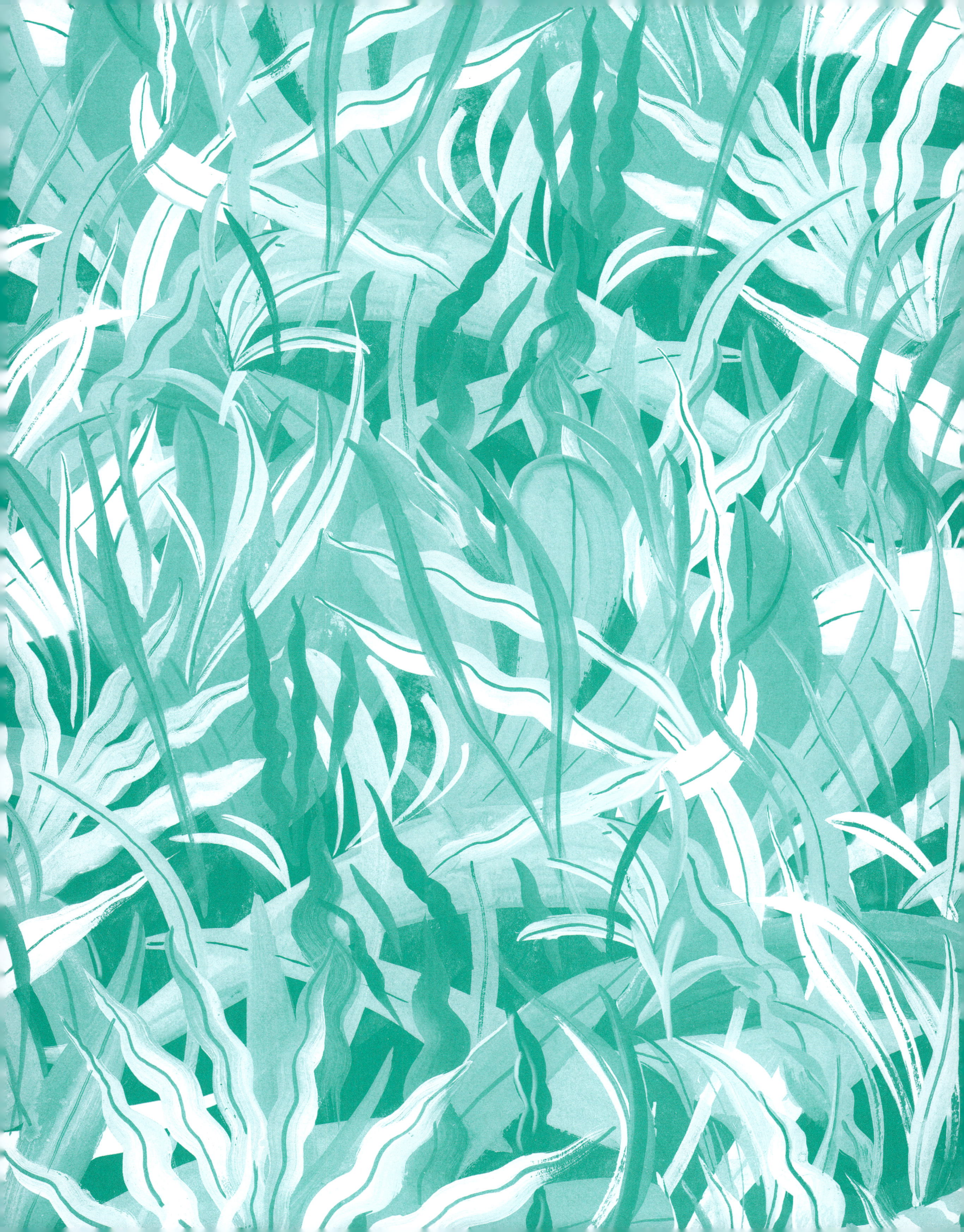

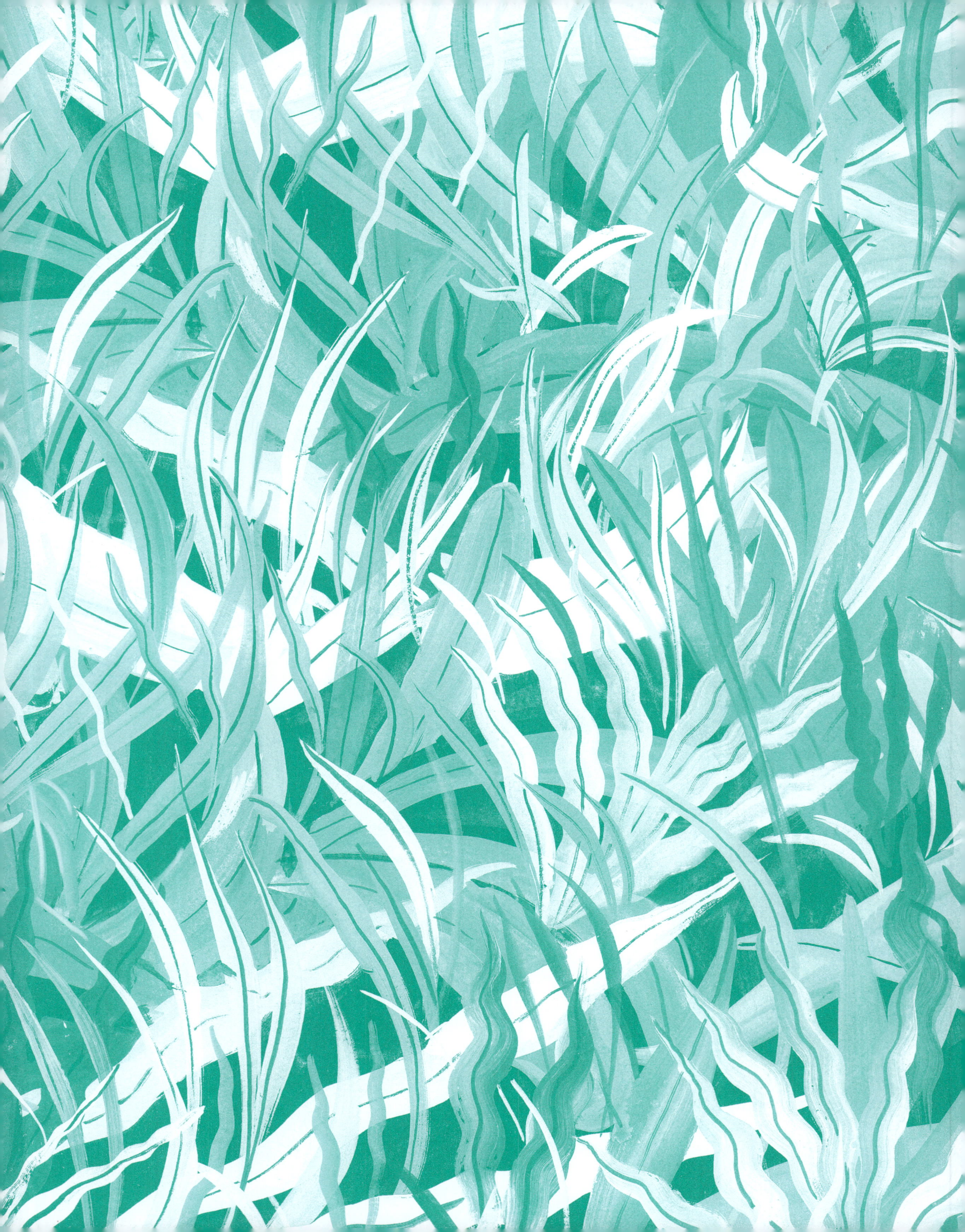